TEN
SECONDS
TO
PEACE

Ten Seconds to Peace

Jeffery Beach

Beach Books
San Francisco

Front and back cover photography by
Jeffery A. Beach

Cover Design by
Jeffery A. Beach & Diane Spencer Hume

Page Design by
Diane Spencer Hume

"*May all mother sentient beings have happiness*
And the causes of happiness.
May they be liberated from suffering
And the causes of suffering.
May they never be separated from the happiness,
Which is free from sorrow.
May they rest in equanimity,
Free from attachment and aversion."

Tibetan Buddhist Prayer

Dear Seeker of Peace,

We live in a time when extended moments of personal peace are hard to come by in daily life. Every moment seems filled with the stresses of every day living. Seldom do we take time out to observe in silence. Yet, if we did, we could achieve, with ease, better performance in all endeavors. To do this, it is crucial to take time-out every day, even if it is a brief moment. Recharging our batteries improves our understanding and perception. Meditating on breath calms the emotions, promoting gentility, compassion, and forgiveness.

As little children, our parents would make us take time out when we got out of control. Even though we were unhappy at the prospect of sitting still, the intended effect of calming us down was achieved, even if for a short time. We are no different as grown-ups. We need to take time out on occasion.

'Take it easy... relax a bit'. It is easy to say, but sometimes very hard to do. There is always a 'good reason' to keep on pushing, yet it is as simple as taking the time to take a few deep breaths. Try this: sit down quietly somewhere, take three, deep, slow, even breaths, pausing briefly at the inhale, and again after exhaling. If you have more time, take more slow easy breaths. Controlled deep breathing helps us to relax and oxygenates our system. It will improve both looks and energy levels, while calming the nervous system.

If more people would try to understand the power of breath, they would make a conscious effort to change their breathing habits. If more people would change their breathing habits, there would be less sickness, more happiness, and more wealth and prosperity on the planet. One cannot breathe deeply, relax, and still feel fear, anger, or other stressful emotions. If you change the way that you breathe, you can change the moment you are in, and that change becomes the next step in your life. If you try deep, slow breathing on a regular basis, a transformation process will automatically begin. At first, the changes are imperceptible. With practice, however, the changes will be like a rebirth through a subtle purification of your body, mind, and speech. There are only two choices in life: Love and Light, or fear and anger. The choice you make is what you are. This is the foundation of all meditation. This is not a hard thing to do. You just have to do it, and with practice, you will integrate meditation into your very being.

Ten Seconds of Peace

Sometimes a few seconds are all we need to get our head on straight, face the next moment, and the next challenge. Emotional stress affects even the best of us. Our minds become clouded and reactive rather than deliberative and focused.

The purpose of this book is to show you how to take time out. Read it through once. Then, choose the exercises that you are most comfortable for you. It takes no more than ten seconds, the 'Ten Seconds of Peace' it takes to read each exercise. Use them daily, and make the time. I say 'make the time', rather than 'when you have time' because it is all too easy to say, "I don't have the time." The more you practice, the greater benefit you will receive. If you

are concerned about some one's welfare, or an-
gered by someone, you can do these exercises
for him or her at the same time as you do them
for yourself. It is a good way to develop gen-
erosity of spirit and a compassionate heart. In
time, your impatience and anger will trans-
form you and the people around you. The
stanzas in this book are meant to be just a be-
ginning for the reader. The variations are infinite. Make up your own visualization and
meditation exercises on the blank pages op-
posing the stanzas, or put drawings, photo-
graphs, do what works for you. I wrote this
book as a reminder for myself as much as any-
one else about the power and benefits of 'taking a moment'.

Learning To Breathe

In a quiet place, sit upright in a chair,
With feet apart flat on the floor,
Your eyes closed.
Take three deep breaths.
Concentrate on your breathing.
Quiet the mind.
Let your thoughts come and go.
Do not hang on to them.
Continue until your breath is full and
regular.
Open your eyes, and continue to
concentrate on your breathing.
Continue to quiet the mind.
Breathing in and breathing out.

When you concentrate on breathing, it will
quiet your mind, and slowly, over time will
silence your fears and anxieties.

Now, in mind, and in heart, offer whatever
benefits and accomplishments you obtain,
for the welfare and happiness of all
humankind, and all life.

Ten
Second
Meditations

Breathing in,
Visualize the full moon in a black ink sky.
Breathing out,
See the moon reflected in a still pond.

Breathing in,
Feel the loving kindness a mother has for
her newborn child.
Breathing out,
Realize you are that newborn child.
Breathing in,
See a stranger who is suffering.
Breathing out,
Radiate that same loving kindness to that
stranger.

Breathing in,
See golden sunlight bathe you in serenity.
Breathing out,
Feel your peace.

Like water mixed with water,
You are one with all.
Breathing in,
Then, breathing out.

*"All things are like
Dreams, illusions, bubbles, shadows...
Like dew drops and a lightning flash,
Contemplate them thus."*

—Diamond Sutra

Letting go of troubles
Is like getting a new life.
It is just returning to
Being you.
Breathing in,
Breathing out.

Take time out:
Slowly, gently, and silently,
Breathe into your abdomen.
Pause.
Slowly, gently, and silently,
Let your breath out through your mouth.
Pause.
Start again.

*"What is the use of worrying about something about which you can do nothing?
And what is the use of worrying about that which you can resolve?"*

—Shantideva

See yourself walking in a garden,
you come upon a most beautiful rose.
Breathing in,
You fully take in its scent.
Breathing out,
You are carefree.

Breathing in,
Feel your breath.
Breathing out,
Suspend your feelings.

Breathing in,
Imagine sitting outdoors,
Listening to a soft wind in the trees.
Breathing out,
Let the wind take your cares away.

Breathing in,
Feel your energy moving up your spine to
the top of your head.
Breathing out,
Move your energy, down the center of your
face, throat, and chest,
To a golden bowl, just below your navel.

Bring your attention
To the space between your eyebrows.
Be in the moment,
See your mind before thought.
Then:
Breathing in,
Fill your body from your toes,
To the top of your head.
Breathing out,
Feel a shower of light
Permeate your surroundings,
And your being.

Breathing in, with eyes closed,
See your inner being as infinite as space.
Breathing out,
See your true nature as compassionate.

Breathe in to your lower abdomen.
Pause.
Then intonate a low tone
As you slowly exhale.
Your troubles will pass.

Slowly Breathe in.
Gently exhaling,
Intone a deep 'Om',
Be that 'Om'.

Inhale, softly,
Bring the breath to a point
Two inches below your navel.
On the Exhale,
Intone the primordial sound 'Ah'.
Fall into Silence and Peace.

Slowly breathe in.
Gently breathing out,
Feel your body.
Merge into the energy
Of your surroundings.

Breathe in,
Hold the breath.
Pay attention to the space within you.
Slowly exhale,
Take longer exhaling than inhaling.
Pay attention to the space outside you.

Breathe in and breathe out
Gently and slowly.
Relax,
See the world as an empty space,
In which your mind plays in all directions.

Breathing in,
Follow your Heart.
Breathing out,
Be open to all possibilities.

Breathing in,
Know your worth.
Breathing out,
Center and Live That Way.

Breathing in,
Follow your breath.
Breathing out,
Follow your breath.
Be still.
Be now.
Awaken in the moment.

See the impermanence of every situation.
All things move on and change.
So now,
Let them go.
Breathing in and breathing out.
Be unattached yet aware.

Breathing in,
Look at your impulse to act.
Stop.
Wait.
Breathing out,
Center yourself.

Breathing in,
Feel your mood.
Breathing out,
Know it is only here for a little while.
Center.
Be undisturbed.

The past is over.
The future never is.
There is only the present to unfold.
Be now,
Be open to myriad possibilities
The Universe has to offer.
While breathing in and breathing out...

It is a warm day.
The sky is a magnificent blue.
Billowing clouds float by
on a gentle breeze.
You are lying down on the bank of a
small, slow moving river.
You are under the shade of a
glorious willow tree.
The willow tree's outer branches dip lightly
into the flowing water.
Breathing in and breathing out...

Breathing in and breathing out,
Your thoughts come and go,
Like swallows in the sky,
Darting here and there.
Observe them and let them go...
Breathing in and breathing out.

Breathing in and breathing out,
Steady your mind.
Breathing in and breathing out,
Now,
Be present.

Breathing in and breathing out,
Focus on being still.
Breathing in and breathing out,
Release yourself.

"If you try to kill all your enemies,
You will never succeed.
But if you kill your anger,
You will have no more enemies."

—Shantideva

Breathing in,
Feel solid as a mountain.
Breathing out,
Be free as space.

While breathing in and out,
See your thoughts as
Ever-changing clouds in the sky.
Let them float by.
Soon the sun will shine.
While breathing in and breathing out.
Nothing is different from that.

Remember a place in your life,
Where you were at joyful peace.
Breathing in:
Be there.
Breathing out.
Let go.
Be in the moment.

Think of your most cherished dream.
Relax, breathe,
Make plans to get there.

This life, this precious human life,
can be over at anytime.
Take nothing for granted.
Be where you want to be.
This is the meaning
of the Native American saying:
"Today is a good day to die."
There are always good reasons
for holding back, but in the end,
You will accomplish less and feel worse,
if you do not follow your heart.

Ask for what you want.
You can do it with prayer.
You can do it with meditation.
Or,
Ask the one
Who can grant your request.
It will set you free.

Breathing in,
Accept your anger.
Be in it,
But not of it.
Breathing out,
Now let it go...

Let go of
Good thoughts.
Disregard
Bad thoughts.
While practicing gentle attention,
Ask for guidance.
You will be answered.

While breathing in and breathing out,
Meditate on the kindness of others.
Focus on that.
Do not focus on their bad intent.
Bad intentions can only give rise to
The same in you.

Sit comfortably, and put your hands,
palms open and facing up on your lap.
Now while breathing in,
slowly make a gentle fist.
Then while breathing out, completely
open your fists without tension.
Do this a few times in a relaxed manner.
You will find your stress vanishing and a
sense of tranquility will pervade your being.
A closed fist holds nothing.
An open hand can hold the world.

Sitting in the sunlight
A quiet moment
This island of silence,
Made somehow possible.

In this bustling city
Breathe in and breathe out.

Breathing in,
We are not here to compete with
One another.
Breathing out,
We are here
To complete
One another.

There is an Arab prayer that says:

"Before we speak a single word,
We should pass through three gates.
The first gatekeeper asks:
'Is it true?'
The second:
'Is it necessary?'
The third gatekeeper asks:
'Is it kind?'"

Breathing in and breathing out....

Sitting comfortably,
and breathing mindfully,
Think of those friends and family you know
who suffer from the turmoil of bad health.

Visualize holding them in your arms,
comforting and loving them,
in the same way
you would wish it for yourself.

Now do the same for those
who create obstacles in your life,
and see them doing the same to you.

Take a moment to sit
quietly and comfortably.
Breathing in and breathing out,
Let your mind drift.
Let your thoughts fly away
like balloons in the deep blue sky...
Bring your mind
back to your breath
and be.

Breathing in,
Say to yourself:
"I am the air."
Breathing out, say:

"Like the breeze
I drift,
Far and wide."

Breathing in,
Tranquility of mind helps me live long.
Breathing out,
Smiling keeps me young.

In your mind,
Remember a joyful, peaceful place...
While breathing in.
Breathing out:
Let it all go.
Feel the present and
Be open to all possibilities.

While breathing in and out,
Bathe yourself in radiant light.
Notice that in that moment,
All your negativities cease their existence.

Breathe in
and
Breathe out.

Breathing in,
Become Present.
Breathing out,
Observe your mind,
Allow it to be
As it is.

Breathing in,
Be now.
Breathing out,
Let go of the notion of time.

My Wish for You

Now that you have read this book, hope fully you will come back to experience some of the exercises. I would also like to urge you to incorporate compassion as a co-practice. Compassionate living must be practiced without discrimination. This means it must be practiced toward the planet and all its residents, whether they are flora and fauna or friend and foe. This is not easy. In time however, it can be achieved with a measure of success. Just look and you will find many in this world at present or in the past, some famous and some known to only a few who are examples for you to emulate.

The greatest reward from compassionate practice is a contagious and energetic serenity that can do much to change the world for the better. Remembering these teachings and sharing them with you is a great privilege for me.

Thank you